DATE DUE

THE
GREAT AMERICAN
BASEBALL
STRIKE

Joe Layden

THE MILLBROOK PRESS
Brookfield, Connecticut

Published by The Millbrook Press
2 Old New Milford Road
Brookfield, CT 06804
© 1995 Blackbirch Graphics, Inc.
First Edition

5 4 3 2 1

Created and produced in association with Blackbirch Graphics.
Series Editor: Tanya Lee Stone

Library of Congress Cataloging-in-Publication Data
Layden, Joe.
    The great American baseball strike/Joe Layden.
    Includes bibliographical references and index.
    Summary: Examines the 1994–95 baseball strike within the context of the history of the game, its past labor problems, and its future as the great American pastime.
    ISBN 1-56294-930-6 (lib. bdg.)
    1. Baseball Strike, 1994–1995—Juvenile literature. [1. Baseball. 2. Baseball Strike, 1994–1995.] I. Title. II. Series.
GV880.17.L39 1995
331.89'281796357'0973—dc20   95-14292
                                                                          CIP
                                                                          AC

Contents

 Chapter One/ Strike! 5

 Chapter Two/ The American Pastime 15

 Chapter Three/ Labor Woes 27

 Chapter Four/ Field of Dreams? 39

 Chapter Five/ As American as Apple Pie 49

Chronology 59

For Further Reading 61

Index 62

Chapter 1

Strike!

Long after the game was over, Oakland Athletics' pitcher Ron Darling was still sitting at his locker. With a bag of ice on his arm, his thoughts centered not on the game he had just lost to the Seattle Mariners, but on whether he would have another chance to pitch that summer. "What do real people do on Labor Day?" he said to a group of reporters. No one had an answer.

Meanwhile, across the hall, in the Mariners' locker room, Ken Griffey, Jr., one of the brightest young stars in the game of professional baseball, found himself talking about the likelihood of a baseball strike instead of about the grand-slam home run he had just hit. "I'm in support of whatever my union tells me to do," Griffey said. "My dad had to go through it, and so do I."

Griffey's father was also a major league ballplayer and, like most players, had experienced the pain and suffering of a labor dispute. Now it was his son's turn.

Three thousand miles away, in New York's Yankee Stadium, a group of fans hung a banner that spoke directly to the warring players and owners: "Y'all come back now, ya hear?" They did not come back, though. Not right away. The next day, on Friday, August 12, 1994, stadiums and locker rooms across North America stood empty.

> For the first time in ninety years, there would be no World Series.

Opposite:
In August 1994, the major league baseball season came to an end. Stadiums across the country stood empty waiting for players and fans to return.

Bags had been packed, and players had departed. The "boys of summer" had traded in their gloves and bats for golf clubs. Some went enthusiastically; most went reluctantly. But, in either case, they were gone. The players, who refused to accept management's proposal of a salary cap (a limit on players' salaries), had gone on strike, and the 1994 season had come to a halt.

It was the beginning of what would turn out to be the longest work stoppage in the history of major league baseball. It pointed out in dramatic detail that baseball was no longer just a game played by talented athletes and enjoyed by millions of fans. It was a very big business.

A Lost Season

One of the saddest aspects of the baseball strike of 1994 was that it came at such a bad time. Professional baseball had been losing some of its magic. No longer was it universally considered to be "America's Game." More and more, that label seemed to apply to other sports. The most recognizable athletes were those in the National Basketball Association (NBA) and the National Football League (NFL). Kids wore sneakers endorsed by Michael Jordan or Shaquille O'Neal. They admired Emmitt Smith and Steve Young. The leisurely pace of baseball seemed increasingly out of place in the fast-paced 1990s.

But 1994 was going to be the year that changed baseball's image. Up until the strike, it had been one of the most compelling seasons in recent history. Several new charismatic stars had emerged: Griffey, Frank "The Big Hurt" Thomas of the Chicago White Sox, and Jeff Bagwell of the Houston Astros, to name a few. A new six-division setup—which had replaced the old four-division one—seemed to be working. Baseball purists had scoffed at the idea of changing the setup, but it resulted in several tight, exciting pennant races. In the Central Division of the American League (AL), for example, only four games

Opposite:
Ken Griffey, Jr., was the son of a former baseball player and a star of the 1994 season. He knew that he would have to wait until the strike was over to resume his career.

separated the top three teams. In the AL West, only five and a half games separated the first-place Texas Rangers and the last-place California Angels.

Not only was it a competitive season, it looked like it would be a record-breaking one. Tony Gwynn of the San Diego Padres had a batting average of .394 at the time of the strike. With only six weeks left in the season, he had a realistic chance of becoming the first player since Ted Williams (in 1941) to hit .400 for the season.

There were power hitters, too. Only three times in the history of the game have two players hit fifty or more home runs in a single season. In 1994, though, Thomas, Griffey, Bagwell, San Francisco's Barry Bonds, and Cleveland's Albert Belle all were on pace to hit fifty. There was also the story of Cal Ripken, Jr., the thirty-three-year-old shortstop for the Baltimore Orioles. By

Cal Ripken, Jr., attempts to tag a runner out. Ripken's chance of breaking the record for most consecutive games played was hurt by the 1994 strike.

June 1995, Ripken may have broken Lou Gehrig's streak of playing in 2,130 consecutive games. Ripken was in the twilight of his career, and every game lost to the strike hurt his chances. "The reality of the situation didn't hit home until this moment," Ripken said, as he cleaned out his locker on August 11. "In a perfect world we'd continue to play, but we're not in a perfect world."

Pitchers had their moments, too. On July 28, Kenny Rogers of the Texas Rangers threw the fourteenth perfect game in baseball history, blanking California, 4–0. Greg Maddux of the Atlanta Braves had a fantastic 1.56 earned-run average for the season.

The strike also ruined a wonderful year for the New York Yankees. Once the greatest team in baseball, the Yankees had fallen on hard times in the previous decade. But in the summer of 1994, they were in first place, looking very much like a team headed for the World Series. Unfortunately, there would be no World Series.

The Issues

The baseball strike was about one thing: money. Over the years, baseball had ceased to be a game played only for fun. In 1984, it was a $600-million business; by 1994 it was a nearly $2-billion industry. In simple terms, the strike occurred because the players and owners could not agree on how to divide the fortune that was being made.

Many observers felt there were no "good guys" or "bad guys" in the strike. Rather, both sides were acting out of greed, and that greed prevented them from negotiating fairly and honestly with each other.

Two key issues led directly to the interruption of the season: revenue sharing and a salary cap. Both issues were open to debate in 1994 because the old contract—known as a collective bargaining agreement—between the players' union and the owners had expired. The players had made tremendous gains in wages through free agency (a player's

PLAYERS' SHARE OF BASEBALL REVENUES

In 1994, players' salaries were expected to be 58% of baseball's total projected revenues of approximately $1.7 billion. The numbers since 1985:

Year	Baseball's Total Revenues	Players' Percentage of Total Revenues
1985	$720,192,000	45%
1986	$798,148,000	45%
1987	$914,109,000	43%
1988	$1,007,474,000	44%
1989	$1,214,833,000	41%
1990	$1,363,605,000	43%
1991	$1,539,217,000	48%
1992	$1,665,106,000	55%
1993	$1,879,737,000	53%

Source: Adapted from *USA Today* Research. By Web Bryant, *USA Today*.

freedom to work for the highest bidder), and they did not want to see that trend come to an end. The owners, on the other hand, wanted to place a league-wide ceiling on the amount of money a player could earn. Salary caps, they argued, existed in the NBA and the NFL, and should exist in baseball as well. Without a cap, they said, salaries would continue to escalate—so high that eventually the league would go broke.

The issue of revenue sharing was related to the salary cap. Without a cap, the owners argued, the richest teams could hire all of the best players and actually buy a championship. And since teams in smaller cities rarely have television contracts that are as lucrative as those in bigger cities, the poor would continue to get poorer, and the rich would get richer. For example, forcing the Yankees and Toronto Blue Jays to share their wealth with smaller teams like the Pittsburgh Pirates and Milwaukee Brewers would distribute the money more evenly. Making the revenue more equal, however, would make it difficult for teams to be able to afford to offer huge contracts to players.

Richard Ravitch, who represented the owners during negotiations, tried to convince the players that they should accept a salary cap and plan for sharing revenue. Donald Fehr, who represented the Major League Players Association, wasted very little time in rejecting that notion. The players, he said, were in opposition to anything that would interfere with their ability to negotiate salaries they felt they had earned.

Almost immediately, the two sides were deadlocked.

A Dark October

It was no accident that the players chose August 12 as their strike deadline. As employees of Major League Baseball, they were salaried workers who by then would have received more than two thirds of their 1994 income. Additionally, they had a strike fund stocked with more than $200 million—a substantial amount of money for the players to live on in the event of a lengthy labor battle.

The owners, however, stood to lose a great deal. A large percentage of their income each year comes in the form of television revenue during the playoffs and World Series—which are held in October. In 1994, broadcast rights to those two events alone were expected to be worth approximately $180 million.

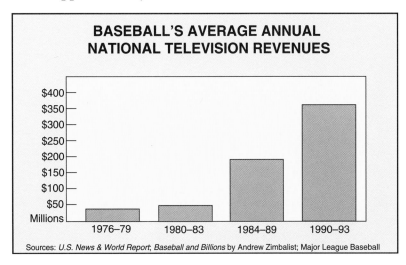

BASEBALL'S AVERAGE ANNUAL NATIONAL TELEVISION REVENUES

Sources: *U.S. News & World Report*; *Baseball and Billions* by Andrew Zimbalist; Major League Baseball

With so much at stake, the players believed that the owners would fold quickly, as they often had in the past. But they did not. Half-hearted negotiations went on for more than a month, with each side refusing to bend. Meanwhile, sports fans began to lose hope that the season could be rescued. They turned their attention to pre-season football.

Finally, on Wednesday, September 14, Milwaukee Brewers president Bud Selig, acting commissioner of baseball, announced the bad news: The season had officially been canceled. There would be no more games. No playoffs. For the first time since 1904, there would be no World Series. A true slice of American culture and tradition, the Series had survived all manner of distractions and terrible events. An earthquake in San Francisco in the fall of 1989 had not stopped the World Series. Even during World War I and World War II, the game went on and the Fall Classic had been played.

At a press conference in September 1994, Bud Selig announces the cancellation of the rest of the baseball season.

Innocent Victims

Financially and emotionally, both the players and owners felt the sting of the baseball strike. So, too, did the fans, whose loyalty to the game was severely tested.

To many observers, however, the real victims of the strike were the thousands of low-income and middle-income workers who suddenly found themselves out of work. One such person was George Rokos, a hot-dog vendor at the SkyDome in Toronto, Canada. "The players make more money in a year than I'll make in my whole life," Rokos told *Sports Illustrated.*

Rokos is a perfect example of the far-reaching effect of the baseball strike. Fans were angered; players lost a portion of their gigantic salaries; owners lost revenue. But when the ballparks went dark, a lot of people lost their jobs. With no games being played, there was no need for hot-dog vendors, or ushers, or parking-lot attendants.

Some clubs also laid off administrative personnel. For example, Bob Pelegrino was dismissed from his job as director of special events for the New York Yankees. Pelegrino and his wife had one small child and another on the way. They had just purchased a new home. For him, the strike was nothing short of a disaster.

It also was devastating for twenty-seven-year-old Adam Monash, a beer vendor at Colorado Rockies games. Monash was saving money to continue his college education. After experiencing firsthand the fallout from the baseball strike, Monash has developed an interest in studying labor relations.

Beer vendors, as well as others whose jobs relied on players taking the field, lost their incomes when the players went on strike.

Stories such as these were common in cities across the country. In Boston, the Red Sox cut 450 employees from their payroll. The Houston Astrodome laid off 1,200 workers. In Baltimore, a bartender lost his job at a pub that relied heavily on fans from nearby Camden Yards. As a sign of protest against the strike, he vowed to live in a tent on the pub's roof for the remainder of the season.

But the game could not withstand an ugly disagreement between labor and management. On the thirty-fourth day of the baseball strike, Selig offered this grim assessment of the situation. "This is a sad day," he said. "Nobody wanted this to happen, but the continuing player strike leaves us no choice but to take this action. We have reached the point where it is no longer practical to complete the remainder of the season or to preserve the integrity of post-season play."

Chapter 2

The American Pastime

Baseball is a game steeped in legend and half-truths. One of the most enduring myths is that the game was invented by a man named Abner Doubleday in the upstate New York village of Cooperstown—which would one day become the home of baseball's Hall of Fame.

In reality, baseball traces its roots back to two British games: cricket, a slow, traditional ball-and-paddle game divided into innings and ruled by umpires; and rounders, a children's game in which a stick and ball were commonly used. Both games were played by early colonists upon their arrival in America, and before long there were multiple variations. The most common was town ball, in which a feeder tossed the ball gently to a striker, who then tried to hit it. By catching the ball on the fly or hitting a runner with the ball, the defensive team recorded an out. And while baseball rules today allow three outs per half inning, only a single out was allowed in town ball.

The Professional Game

The first baseball team was born on September 23, 1845, when a group of twenty-eight men from the Knickerbocker Volunteer Fire Company formed the New York Knickerbocker Base Ball Club. They were, for the most part, wealthy men in search of a new sport.

Baseball's popularity grew dramatically in the 1920s.

Opposite:
In 1869, the Cincinnati Red Stockings became the first professional baseball team. Fans were charged admission to see their games and the players received salaries.

The New York Knickerbockers formed the first baseball club in 1845.

One of the players, Alexander Cartwright, along with team president Daniel Lucius Adams, wrote a new set of rules that permanently shaped the game. It was the Knickerbockers who established that the infield would be shaped like a diamond and that runners should be tagged out or thrown out, rather than hit with the ball.

    For more than two decades, baseball was a game played exclusively for recreational purposes. In 1869, the first all-professional team, the Cincinnati Red Stockings, took the field—and baseball officially became a business.

    The Red Stockings team was the brainchild of Harry Wright, the son of a professional cricket player. It was

Loss of Innocence

In the fall of 1919, baseball was rocked by an incident known as The Black Sox Scandal. It began with a meeting between first baseman Chick Gandil of the Chicago White Sox and Joseph "Sport" Sullivan, a gambler who often relied on Gandil for inside information about injured players. This time, though, Gandil had something bigger on his mind: For $100,000, he told Sullivan, he and some of his teammates would make sure the White Sox lost the World Series.

The White Sox were an angry, bitter team. The players were poorly paid in comparison to other teams—a fact that irritated them tremendously, especially since they were so successful on the field. Eventually, Gandil attempted to convince seven players to go along with the scheme: pitchers Claude "Lefty" Williams and Eddie Cicotte; outfielder Happy Felsch; infielders Swede Risberg, Fred McMullin, and Buck Weaver; and perhaps the greatest hitter who ever lived, Joe Jackson.

The White Sox lost the Series, but the conspirators received only a portion of the money they had expected. Jackson insisted he had never agreed to go along with the plot, and even sent a letter to owner Charles Comiskey afterward, asking what he should do with the $5,000 he had received. Over the next year, rumors of a fix spread through the media, and, in September 1920, a grand jury began to investigate allegations that the White Sox had thrown the 1919 World Series.

With the help of signed testimony from Jackson and Cicotte, all eight players were indicted for conspiracy. But none was convicted. The transcripts of their confessions disappeared, and all eight players were acquitted for lack of evidence. But they never played professional baseball again: Shortly after the acquittal, baseball commissioner Kenesaw Mountain Landis imposed a lifetime ban on all eight players—including Buck Weaver, who maintained his innocence until the day he died.

Claude "Lefty" Williams and Eddie Cicotte were two of the eight Chicago White Sox players involved in The Black Sox Scandal.

Wright who realized that Americans were willing to pay good money for entertainment. They happily handed over 50 cents to see a theatrical presentation. Surely they would do the same for a good baseball game, which, he reasoned, was far more entertaining.

Wright not only charged admissions for games; he also paid each of his players a salary. For the first time, it was possible for a person to earn a living playing baseball. The Red Stockings won sixty-five games in 1869; they did not lose any. Their profit for the year was exactly $1.39.

Glory Days

Baseball was a pitcher's game in the first two decades of the twentieth century—mainly because the pitcher was allowed to do almost anything to the ball. He could spit on it, scuff it, scratch it with his cleats. All of these things tended to make the ball move unpredictably when it was thrown toward the plate, which gave the pitcher a huge advantage over the batter.

By 1920, it was against the rules to "doctor" the baseball, and the focus had switched from the pitcher to the batter. The 1920s saw baseball's popularity increase dramatically, thanks to the arrival of several new hitting stars. By far the most famous of these men was George Herman Ruth, who came to be known simply as The Babe.

Babe Ruth started out as a pitcher with the Boston Red Sox, but when he was sold to the New York Yankees in 1920, he turned his attention to hitting. And what a hitter he was—arguably the greatest in history. In his first season with the Yankees, Babe Ruth hit fifty-four home runs. He became a huge celebrity. Thanks to him, the Yankees drew more than a million fans in a single season for the first time.

Ruth remains the biggest star baseball has ever known. In 1927, he hit sixty home runs in a single season—a record that stood for more than three decades. Because

During the 1920s and
1930s, George Herman
"Babe" Ruth was celebrated
for his incredible talent as a
home-run hitter.

of his fame as a home-run hitter, Ruth was often referred to as The Sultan of Swat.

He was not the only great hitter of his time, though. Ruth's teammate, Lou Gehrig, and Rogers Hornsby of the St. Louis Cardinals, were other offensive stars of this period. Gehrig, who was nicknamed "Iron Horse," batted .300 or more for twelve straight years. Hornsby had a .400 average during five consecutive years of his career. The 1920s were considered to be one of the brightest eras the game has ever known.

Lou Gehrig's great hitting career with the New York Yankees lasted fourteen years. Gehrig set many records, including most consecutive games played.

Breaking the Color Barrier

In the summer of 1945, Branch Rickey, president and general manager of the Brooklyn Dodgers, invited a young black man named Jack Roosevelt Robinson to his office. Jackie Robinson was twenty-six years old at the time. He had been a multi-sport star at UCLA. Later, as a lieutenant in the army, he earned a reputation as a troublemaker because he refused to go along with racial segregation policies.

An immensely talented athlete, Robinson was shortstop for the Kansas City Monarchs, a member of baseball's Negro leagues. Although not the finest black player of his time, Robinson was a very good baseball player and a well-educated, articulate, strong-willed man. In Rickey's eyes, Robinson was the ideal choice to break baseball's long tradition of barring black players.

Rickey conducted a lengthy interview with Robinson to make sure he understood the hardships that awaited him. He would be the subject of racial slurs. On and off the field, he would be taunted and harassed. Robinson already knew all of this. He agreed to play, and two months later, on October 23, he signed a contract for the 1946 season and was assigned to the Dodgers' minor league team in Montreal, Canada.

Robinson's debut came on April 18, 1946, when he played second base for the Royals in a game against the Jersey City Giants. He performed impressively, hitting a home run and three singles, and stealing two bases in a 14–1 victory. Robinson went on to lead the International League in hitting that year with a .349 average.

In 1947, he was summoned to the majors. Many people, including some of his own teammates, were cruel to him. He endured threats and insults. On April 15, at Ebbets Field in Brooklyn, against the Boston Braves, Jackie Robinson became the first black player to appear in a major league baseball game. He started at first base.

The Negro Leagues

It was not until 1947, when Jackie Robinson took first base for the Brooklyn Dodgers, that an African American was allowed to play major league baseball. There was, however, a place where black men could hone their skills and receive salaries for their efforts: the Negro leagues.

The first of these was created in 1920, when Rube Foster formed the Negro National League (NNL). The NNL consisted of eight teams that played a sixty- to eighty-game schedule. The success of that league prompted the formation of a second league—the Eastern Colored League (ECL)—in 1923. One year later, the champions of the two leagues met in the first black World Series.

The ECL folded in 1929, and was replaced by the American Negro League (ANL), which lasted only one year. Following the stock market crash of October 1929, the NNL also began to struggle (as did many white teams). By 1932, as the United States fell deeper into the Great Depression, the worst economic crisis it has ever known, the NNL was out of business. One year later, though, it reappeared. From 1933 through 1936, the NNL was the only black professional league. It was primarily an eastern league, with franchises in cities such as Pittsburgh, Philadelphia, New York, Baltimore, and Newark. A second black organization—the Negro American League (NAL)—was formed in 1936, and for several years both leagues did reasonably well. Players earned $2,000 to $3,000 per year—less than white players were paid in the majors, but far more than African Americans typically made during the Depression.

Over the years, historians have often reflected on the talent displayed in the Negro leagues. Some of the greatest players in the game spent their entire careers in the Negro leagues. Among the best was Leroy Satchel Paige, who in 1933 compiled a record believed to have been 31 wins, 4 losses. In his long career, he won an estimated 2,000 games—four times the major league record. It is also worth noting that black teams played white teams at least 438 times in exhibition games. Blacks won 309 of those contests.

Satchel Paige had an impressive baseball career playing for the Negro leagues.

Jackie Robinson was the first African American to play major league baseball. At the onset of his career he had to withstand harsh criticism from fans and teammates because of his race.

Despite all of the difficulty he faced, Robinson batted .297 that year and led the National League in stolen bases. The *Sporting News* named him National League Rookie of the Year.

Thanks to Jackie Robinson, the door was open for players of all races, and baseball would no longer be only a white man's game.

A League of Their Own

In 1943, Phillip Wrigley, king of the chewing gum empire, came up with a plan to bring baseball to a wider audience and to sustain interest during World War II. At the time, more than 40,000 women were playing softball in amateur and semi-pro leagues. It was Wrigley's idea to bring the best of them together in a single, professional league—and exchange the softball for a baseball.

After tryouts in Chicago in the spring of 1943, the All-American Girls Professional Baseball League was formed. There were four teams: the Rockford Peaches, Racine Belles, Kenosha Comets, and South Bend Blue Sox. The women were talented athletes, but under Wrigley's orders, they also had to conduct themselves in a way that he considered feminine. That meant they had to wear skirts, rather than pants, when they played. Off the field, they were required to wear skirts, high heels, and makeup. If any player failed to adhere to the dress code, she was fined. Wrigley even hired a cosmetics company to conduct a "charm school" for his women players.

If Wrigley's notions about sports and femininity seem outdated, they were nothing short of brilliant at the time. The All-American Girls Professional Baseball League grew rapidly; at its peak, in 1948, it consisted of ten teams and drew nearly a million fans. Eventually, though, mismanagement, the growth of television, and the increasingly popular belief that women should not be playing sports contributed to the death of the All-American League. It folded in 1954.

The Rockford Peaches were one of the four original teams to make up the All-American Girls Professional Baseball League.

Chapter 3

Labor Woes

The sport of baseball is no stranger to labor unrest. In fact, the relationship between owners and players has almost always been a fragile one, marked by tension and mistrust. Professional baseball players today want essentially the same thing pro athletes wanted a century earlier: to be paid what they believe they are worth. Similarly, the goal of management remains basically unchanged: to keep the high cost of doing business to a minimum.

The two sides need each other, of course. They are a team, united in purpose. They want to win baseball games, attract fans to their ballparks, and make money. But they disagree on how that money should be divided.

In the latter part of the nineteenth century, when the sport was still in its infancy, it was common for baseball players to jump from team to team. They routinely took part in a process known as revolving, which meant they would offer their services to the highest bidder before the start of each season. To both players and owners, this earliest form of free agency seemed a fair way to do business. If a player performed well on the field, he was

Baseball has survived many strikes in the past twenty-five years.

Opposite:
In 1885, John Montgomery Ward—a player for the New York Giants—formed the first union for professional baseball players.

rewarded with a bigger contract the next year; if he performed badly, there would be less interest from competing clubs, and he would be forced to accept a lower salary.

Salaries, however, began to increase at an alarming rate, and owners became wary of revolving. In 1880, citing an urgent need to protect the game from financial ruin, owners in the National League of Professional Base Ball Clubs decided to take action. They instituted a reserve clause in players' contracts that tied a player to a specific team for the duration of his career. No longer could a star player shop around for a new team at the end of a season; instead, he was forced to accept whatever salary he was offered—or find a different line of work. In effect, the owners became true owners: The players were their property. A player could switch to a different team only if he was traded, or released from his contract, by his previous owner. At first, the reserve clause applied only to a handful of players on each team, but by 1883 it was a standard part of every contract.

This move, which represented the death of free agency, angered the players, who felt as though they had been stripped of their freedom. The owners disagreed. They believed the reserve clause was not only fair, but necessary. The split between labor and management was officially established, and the groundwork for the first players' union had been laid.

The Players League

In 1885, New York Giants shortstop John Montgomery Ward, an outspoken and intelligent critic of the reserve clause, helped found the Brotherhood of Professional Base Ball Players. "There was a time when the National League stood for integrity and fair dealing," Ward wrote. "Today it stands for dollars and cents.... Players have been bought, sold and exchanged as though they were sheep instead of American citizens."

The owners responded quickly to this first attempt at a players' organization. Instead of discussing the new union's concerns, the owners tried to take greater control of the game by implementing a salary cap. In 1889, they declared that no player would make more than $2,500 in a single season, regardless of his productivity. Owners provoked additional bitter feelings by insisting that the players pay a rental fee for their uniforms. The dispute then turned ugly. A group of fifty-six players, led by Ward, revolted against management. They abandoned their contracts, left their teams, and, with the aid of several wealthy businessmen, formed a new league.

The Players League, which featured many of the National League's finest players—including Mike "King" Kelly, the biggest star of that era—did fairly well at first. The new league had some first-rate athletes, as well as the backing of the American Federation of Labor. It also had a lot of confidence. The Players League deliberately established franchises (the independent right of membership in a professional sports league) in cities that were already occupied by the National League. Their plan was to force fans to choose between the two leagues: the new Players League, which featured established stars; or the National League, whose rosters were dotted with aging ballplayers who had been lured out of retirement, and other replacement players.

As it turned out, the Players League underestimated the strength and determination of the National League owners. Both leagues conducted full seasons in 1890, and, while the Players League had better attendance figures, it was the National League that survived. (The American Association also had a full season in 1890. This league was formed in 1882 by owners of big-city clubs that had been rejected by the National League.) Investors in the Players League withdrew their support, and many players were convinced to return to their old teams. Shortly after the end of the season, representatives of the Players

The Salary Story

When the first professional baseball team—the Cincinnati Red Stockings—was formed in 1869, the highest-paid player earned $1,400. His name was George Wright, and in that initial season he batted .519 and hit 59 home runs.

Today, the minimum salary is $109,000, and players with far less impressive statistics than George Wright's routinely make salaries of $1 million. In 1994, the average salary of a major league baseball player was $1.2 million; more than 100 players earned at least $3 million. The highest-paid player was Bobby Bonilla, of the New York Mets, whose contract was worth $6.3 million per season. Based on his 1993 performance, Bonilla received approximately $13,400 per hit.

One of the greatest players in history, Babe Ruth, had an $80,000 contract in 1930—lavish compared to the league's average salary of $7,000, but a small sum when compared to the contracts of the 1990s. Today, a player of Ruth's stature would be worth millions of dollars per year. Not only was he a tremendous baseball player, but he also was an entertainer—a man who attracted fans to the ballpark with his personality as well as his athleticism.

As teams openly bid for the services of the best player, salaries began to increase with the advent of free agency in the mid-1970s. But it was not until much later, with the help of increased revenue from television contracts, that the most dramatic changes took place. For example, Wright's salary in 1869 was roughly seven times greater than that of the average American worker. In 1976, major league baseball players earned eight times more than the average worker.

From 1984 to 1994, however, salaries increased by more than 368 percent. Today, the average player's salary is 50 times greater than that of the average American worker. The widening of that gap has made it difficult for the fan to feel much sympathy for the modern ballplayer—even during a strike. As Rufus Ziegler, a cook at the Houston Astrodome, told *Newsweek*, "Cat out there making $2 million thinks he needs more money? What he needs is a new life."

AVERAGE MAJOR LEAGUE SALARIES
1984–1994

Source: Major League Baseball Players Association

League and the National League met and decided that the country could not support both organizations.

The Players League was absorbed (as was the American Association one year later), and its union was destroyed. Players who had taken part in the uprising were told that their actions would not be held against them. Many returned to their old teams, hopeful that the owners would fulfill their promise to improve working conditions. The reserve clause and salary cap, however, remained in effect. Things remained relatively quiet until 1954.

Free Agency

In 1954, a group of player representatives voted to form the Major League Baseball Players Association (MLBPA). But it was not until 1966, when Marvin Miller—an expert in the art of labor negotiations—was hired, that anyone considered the MLBPA to be a true union. Led by Miller, the players won a series of minor victories. Through baseball's first collective bargaining agreement in 1968, they received higher minimum salaries, better health insurance plans, and increases in retirement benefits.

There was still, however, unhappiness among the players over the issue of free agency. One player at the center of this controversy was Curt Flood, an outfielder for the St. Louis Cardinals. Flood was one of the best players in the game, and at the end of the 1968 season, after having led the Cardinals to a second consecutive National League pennant, he asked for a $30,000 raise. The request angered St. Louis owner August Busch, who publicly scolded Flood for being greedy.

One year later, when Flood's contract had expired, Busch announced that he was trading his star outfielder to the Philadelphia Phillies. Flood was enraged. He did not wish to move his family. He was thirty-one years old and wanted to finish his career in St. Louis. So, on December 24, 1969, he wrote a letter to baseball commissioner Bowie Kuhn, asking that he be declared a free agent. Kuhn, using the reserve clause as an explanation, denied the request.

Flood did not give up. He felt he had earned the freedom to offer his services to the highest bidder, and he promised to take his case to the Supreme Court of the United States. The fight lasted several years. Flood put his career on hold and spent most of his time in court. Some players were on his side; others were not. Fans, generally speaking, had little sympathy, which Flood understood. "I was telling my story to deaf ears," he said.

Marvin Miller helped MLBPA members gain some control over decisions regarding their major league careers.

Curt Flood fought all the way to the Supreme Court to become a free agent. Flood lost his fight, but he paved the way for other players to have the right to veto any undesired trade.

"To a person who would give their firstborn child to be doing what I was doing. And he just could not understand how there could possibly be anything wrong with baseball."

In October 1972, the Supreme Court ruled against Flood. Publicity over the case, however, prompted fearful owners to make some concessions. They agreed to give any player with ten or more years of experience—including five with his current team—the right to veto any trade.

Also in 1972, following a thirteen-day players' strike, Miller negotiated a deal in which team owners agreed to impartial binding arbitration of salary disputes. In simple terms, this meant that a player whose contract had expired no longer had to accept whatever salary was offered. He could ask for more, and if an arbitrator ruled in his favor, the owner would be forced to either pay that amount or grant the player an unconditional release. In 1974, pitcher Jim "Catfish" Hunter used arbitration to earn his release from the Oakland Athletics. As soon as he became a free agent, Hunter found that every team in baseball wanted him on its roster. He eventually signed with the New York Yankees for more than $1 million per year— easily the richest contract the sport had ever seen.

The case of Catfish Hunter led to the inevitable crumbling of the reserve clause and the beginning of free agency. In 1975, a landmark arbitration panel declared that pitchers Andy Messersmith and Dave McNally—two men who had each played a single season without a contract—were free agents. The panel also ruled that any player with six years of major league experience had the right to file for free agency. Baseball, as a business, had permanently changed.

Catfish Hunter smiles after officially joining the New York Yankees in 1974. His arbitration case helped other players win free agency.

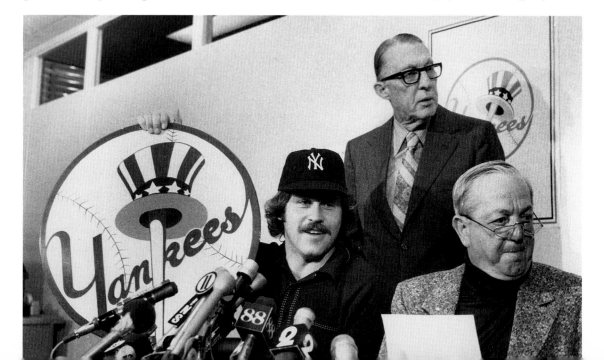

Picket Lines

The baseball strike of 1994 was notable primarily because of its length: Never before had a work stoppage forced the postponement of the World Series. But baseball had survived many strikes in the past twenty-five years. The strike of 1994, for example, was the eighth time since 1972 that the game had been interrupted because of a labor dispute.

Comparatively speaking, the strike of '72, which occurred during collective bargaining negotiations, was brief, lasting less than two weeks and causing the cancellation of only eighty-six games. Still, it had an obvious effect on the game. Pete Rose, a star player for the Cincinnati Reds at the time, has noted that it probably cost him a chance for a 200-hit season (he ended up with 198).

In 1976, during another round of collective bargaining negotiations, it was the owners' turn to play hardball. They locked out the players during spring training, hoping

Bowie Kuhn responds to questions about a pending strike during a press conference in Boston in 1969. As commissioner, Kuhn tried to mediate problems between players and owners.

that such a move would cause the players to panic and accept a quick settlement. Commissioner Kuhn stepped in after seventeen days and ordered the training camps to be reopened and negotiations continued. The season began on time, and a settlement was reached in July. The players, who had threatened to strike just as they had done in 1972, were pleased with the new union contract, which again gave them better retirement plans and higher minimum salaries.

By 1980, both the players and owners were interested in changing the free agent system. The players, who had become quite wealthy in the new open market, wanted even greater flexibility. Specifically, they did not like the idea of having to wait six years before declaring free agency. The owners, meanwhile, were more concerned about being compensated for the players they lost to free agency. They wanted to receive either cash or new players for each player they lost to free agency. The two sides were miles apart in negotiations during spring training, and the players threatened to strike if an agreement was not reached by May 22, 1980. At the last minute, however, a strike was averted, and the season went on. The ill will, however, continued.

On June 11, 1981—two months into the regular season, the players decided to strike again. Again, free agency was at the center of the debate. The players claimed that the owners' demands for compensation would make teams reluctant to bid for free agents and thus reduce their earning power. The owners, who had a $50 million strike insurance policy, tried to break the union. But it did not work. After seven weeks—and the cancellation of 712 games—the owners gave up. The players returned to the field, still holding a firm grip on free agency.

There were other problems in the 1980s and 1990s, though nothing as grim as the strikes of 1981 and 1994. In 1985, for instance, a walkout lasted only two days.

Baseball and Antitrust Laws

In 1913, a group of businessmen got together and decided to form a third professional baseball league, one that would compete in the market-place against the American and National leagues. Owners in the new league (the Federal League) tried to sign players from the American and National leagues by offering them more money. Organized baseball fought some of the players who tried to move by taking them to court and arguing that they had broken their contracts. In 1915, the Federal League filed a lawsuit against baseball in which it claimed that the American and National leagues formed an illegal monopoly in restraint of free trade (antitrust). This, the Federal League argued, represented a violation of the Sherman Antitrust Act of 1890 (an act that prohibited restraint of free trade among states or within foreign nations).

The case was eventually settled out of court, and the Federal League was dissolved after its owners received a large cash payment. However, investors in one team, the Baltimore Federals, wanted to deal to include an option to buy an existing team—the St. Louis Cardinals—and move it to another city. The request was denied, and another antitrust suit was filed. A judge in Washington, D.C., first ruled that baseball *was* in violation of antitrust laws. But in 1922, the decision was reversed by the Supreme Court of the United States. Associate Justice Oliver Wendell Holmes, Jr., determined that although baseball was a business, the act of staging games for profit was "not trade or commerce in the commonly-accepted use of those words."

Since then, professional baseball has been in the unique position of being exempt from federal antitrust laws. This is not true of the National Basketball Association, the National Hockey League, or the National Football League.

In February 1995, senators Orrin Hatch of Utah and Daniel Patrick Moynihan of New York introduced a bill in Congress that proposed an end to baseball's exemption from antitrust laws as they apply to labor negotiations. Under the terms of the bill, if the major league owners tried to change any of the work rules within the sport, the players would have the right to challenge those changes in court. The move was designed not only to help force an end to the then six-month-old baseball strike, but to address what many observers felt was an unfair exemption.

"Baseball is the only sport that has an antitrust exemption," Hatch said. "[Congress] has allowed a fiction to exist in order to protect the leagues and the owners."

Congressmen Orrin Hatch (left) and Robert Graham (right) discuss a proposed bill that would have brought an end to the baseball strike.

In 1981, twelve-year-old David Divito participated in a candlelight vigil outside of Wrigley Field in Chicago. He and other fans were angry about the cancellation of the All-Star game and the ongoing strike.

And in 1989, the owners were found guilty of conspiring against the players by agreeing not to bid on free agents. They were ordered to pay all players who were affected a total of $10.5 million in lost wages.

All of these developments settled nothing and only served to increase the tension and mistrust between the owners and players. By the summer of 1994, the stage was set for the longest labor dispute in the history of major league baseball.

Field of Dreams?

Octtober 1994 came and went. For the first time in ninety years, there was no World Series. Fall turned to winter, and the strike of 1994 became the strike of 1995.

Along the way, hostility increased between the players and owners, who still had not agreed on a new collective bargaining contract. Talks resumed, then broke off, then resumed again . . . and broke off again.

In December 1994, the owners made good on a threat to impose a salary cap—with or without the players' approval. This move, however, served only to heighten the tension and make the possibility of a settlement more remote.

Less than a month later, when it became apparent that the salary cap was an issue that would forever stand in the way of an agreement, the owners backed off. The cap was withdrawn. But at the same time, the owners decided to make other changes in the way they had traditionally done business with players. One change they made was the elimination of salary arbitration, which they believed was primarily responsible for the rapidly rising salaries of players. In response, the players filed a charge of unfair labor practice with the National Labor Relations Board.

Empty stadiums at games played by replacement players showed fans' opinions of the strike.

Opposite:
W. J. Usery, a federal mediator appointed by President Bill Clinton, tried to negotiate a strike settlement between players and owners. Here, he talks about the end of the 1994 baseball season during a press conference.

The Commissioner

In the wake of the infamous Black Sox Scandal of 1919, in which eight members of the Chicago White Sox were accused of accepting money to throw the World Series, it was determined that baseball needed a strong leader. The owners dissolved the three-man National Commission that had previously overseen the game, and adopted the idea of a single, powerful commissioner.

Many candidates were considered for the post, including former president William Howard Taft. After much debate, though, the owners selected Judge Kenesaw Mountain Landis. He wasted little time in putting his stamp on the game. The day after the eight Chicago players were acquitted of conspiracy and fraud charges, Landis banned them all from baseball for life. With that single historic gesture, he legitimized the power of the commissioner's office.

At the time of the 1995 baseball strike, however, the office of the commissioner was empty. In 1992, the owners had forced commissioner Fay Vincent out of office. Their reasons were vague, but critics of the move suggested that the owners were simply setting the stage for the next round of negotiations with the players. A strong commissioner would stand in the middle of the war and make sure both sides acted sensibly. He would put the interests of the game and the fans ahead of the interests of the owners or players.

With the post vacant, Bud Selig took on the duties of the commissioner, supposedly on a temporary basis. Three years later, however, Selig was still the "acting commissioner." This irked the players because Selig was also the president of the Milwaukee Brewers and, presumably, on the side of management. Selig openly defended his lengthy stay in the role of interim commissioner by saying he did not want an outsider deciding a private labor issue.

Unfortunately, the players and owners—equally stubborn—repeatedly showed they were incapable of settling the matter themselves.

"I don't think there would be a strike right now if there was a commissioner," noted Peter Ueberroth, himself a former commissioner. "It would be over within 24 hours."

Acting commissioner Bud Selig (seated) and player representative Donald Fehr (standing) take a break during congressional hearings about the strike.

By February 1, 1995, the opening of spring training was only two weeks away, and there was little cause for optimism. Even W. J. Usery, the federal mediator appointed to help settle the dispute, expressed only disappointment.

Meanwhile, public opinion polls reflected the anger of American baseball fans, who felt that the players and the owners were equally responsible. Clearly, the strike had become a public relations nightmare for the sport of baseball. And it was about to get even worse.

Silent Spring

As the beginning of spring training drew near, there was increased pressure—from the public, the media, and even from the president of the United States—to settle the strike. The fear, of course, was that if the owners and players failed to reach an agreement by February 16—the day training camps were scheduled to open—another season would be threatened.

President Bill Clinton told U.S. Labor Secretary Robert Reich that he wanted the dispute settled in time for spring training. Nevertheless, negotiations continued at a very slow pace, with virtually no progress being made.

By February 1, the owners were talking seriously about opening training camps—with or without major league players. They said they would find replacement players to fill out their rosters, and spring training would be conducted as usual. This threat served only to anger the Major League Players Association, whose members dug in deeper. They decided they would call the owners' bluff. To them, and to many outside observers, the prospect of replacement baseball was absurd. Where would the players come from? And who would pay to see them? It was ridiculous, the players told themselves. Surely the owners would not stoop to that level.

The very prospect of replacement baseball prompted a series of emotional reactions, some of which demonstrated

President Clinton discusses the strike during a press conference in February 1995. Clinton wanted the strike settled in time for spring training.

that the owners were not entirely united. The Toronto Blue Jays, for example, barred manager Cito Gaston and his staff from working with replacement players. Baltimore Orioles owner Peter Angelos called replacement baseball "a mockery," and said his team would not use replacement players during the regular season even if the American League fined or suspended him.

"The use of replacement players is a terrible disservice to major league baseball and to the fans of professional baseball," Angelos said. "What is happening in the quest for 'pick-up' players to serve as so-called 'replacement players' makes a mockery of major league baseball and diminishes the stature and integrity of the game in a manner which, to the Orioles, is thoroughly unacceptable."

On February 7, federal mediator W. J. Usery issued a series of recommendations intended to move the talks forward, including a reduction in the amount of time a player had to spend in the league before being eligible for free agency.

Both the players and owners rejected the plan. Two weeks later, spring training began with replacement players.

The Replacements

Only once before had replacement players ever taken the field in professional baseball. On May 18, 1912, the Detroit Tigers used eight replacement players during the first strike in baseball history. The Tigers players had walked out because the American League refused to re-instate their best player, Ty Cobb, after Cobb had been

Replacement player Rick Hirtensteiner loses his glove when he tries to catch a ball during a Toronto Blue Jays spring training game. Replacement players were not as skilled or athletic as the striking professionals.

suspended for climbing into the stands and attacking a heckler. The Tigers went out to local sandlots and offered a shot at the big-time to a handful of starry-eyed young men. The replacement team also included Tigers scouts Joe Sugden and Deacon Jim McGuire, both of whom were in their forties. The team played one game, against the Philadelphia Athletics, and lost by a score of 24–2.

In 1995, the replacements got a bit more time to strut their stuff. Training camps opened as scheduled, with most teams fielding a combination of minor league players and true replacements—men who just a few days earlier had been playing in recreation leagues. A few major leaguers threatened to report to camp, but none did. The players remained united. Meanwhile, their roster spots were temporarily occupied by overweight, out-of-shape players chasing a dream. Among the replacements was twenty-nine-year-old Juan Velasquez, a catcher who had not played competitively for three years. Velasquez took a leave of absence from his job selling satellite dishes. To him, the decision to be a strikebreaker, as the replacements were unkindly termed, was a practical one: He wanted to make more money to provide better care for his three children.

In general, the replacements were poorly skilled. Television highlights from spring training usually consisted of a series of dropped fly balls, muffed grounders, and wild pitches. Some managers, like the Cardinals' Joe Torre, tried to maintain a sense of humor about the situation. Others, like Detroit's Sparky Anderson, thought it was no laughing matter. He walked away from his job on the first day of training camp, saying he would not return until the strike was over.

"I've always wondered if something really important came up, could I stand up?" Anderson told *Sports Illustrated*. "I didn't know. I'd never had to. This time, I *had* to. What [baseball owners] are doing with replacement players is absolutely ridiculous."

Opposite:
Sparky Anderson refused to coach replacement players. He felt that the owners were being "ridiculous" in their use of inadequate players.

The Only Show

If the baseball strike was a disaster for major league players, owners, fans, and vendors, it was a boost for at least one group of people: those involved with minor league teams.

The quality of play in Class A, Class AA, and Class AAA ball is obviously lower than it is in the major leagues. The players are not quite as fast, they do not hit the ball as far or as consistently, they commit more errors, and the pitchers do not throw as hard. Still, in places like Pittsfield, Massachusetts (home of the Single A Mets), Buffalo, New York (home of the Triple A Bisons) and Pawtucket, Rhode Island (home of the Triple A Red Sox), fans turned out to watch baseball in the summer of 1994. For a little more than a month, they were the only game in town.

Although the strike did not translate into record-setting attendance at all minor league parks, it did give minor league players an opportunity to perform in the spotlight. To some fans, the change was refreshing. In the minors, the players are not millionaires. They are kids, playing because they love the game. They are not spoiled. The game at this level is small and personal. Fans can chat with ballplayers around the batting cage. They can get a good seat for less than five dollars. Going to a minor league game is inexpensive entertainment for the entire family.

And, for a change, it suggests something good about the game of baseball. As Pawtucket manager Buddy Bailey said, "At least somebody's willing to play ball."

Fans at a Ravens game in New Haven, Connecticut, enjoy the action on the small, intimate field of the minor league team.

The Detroit Tigers then found a replacement manager in Thom Runnells, the coach of the club's minor league franchise in Trenton, New Jersey.

The Fans Speak Out

The owners knew what to expect out of replacement baseball. In 1987, they had watched the National Football League (NFL) use replacement players for three weeks during the nastiest strike in that sport's history. Public response to replacement football was, at best, lukewarm. The quality of play was poor, and attendance was dismal.

So, owners guessed that few people would pay to watch replacement players stage exhibition baseball games. Most teams were smart enough to substantially lower the price of admission to games—some charged as little as a dollar. The economies of the states of Florida and Arizona, the primary training sites for most clubs, were severely hurt by the strike. A lot of baseball fans plan their vacation schedules around spring training. This year, however, the pace of life in towns such as Winter Haven and Vero Beach, Florida, was noticeably slower.

At Dodgertown (the name of the Los Angeles Dodgers' spring training complex), where hundreds of fans usually watch practice each day, and thousands pay to see exhibition games, the stands were empty. In the Dodgers' first home pre-season game, against the Detroit Tigers, paid attendance was 3,079. This does not sound bad until you realize that 2,500 of those seats belonged to season ticket holders, most of whom had not shown up. Actual attendance was estimated at close to 2,000. By comparison, the 1993 spring training opener drew a crowd of 6,408. Even worse was the Dodgers' first away game in Fort Lauderdale a week earlier, against the Yankees. For that game, only 500 fans showed up.

Clearly, the fans had spoken. They were not going to accept replacement baseball as the real thing.

Chapter 5

As American as Apple Pie

Baseball has often been referred to as The American Pastime. But what does that really mean? It means that, more than any other sport, baseball reflects our heritage and our culture. Consider the following passage, written by the poet Walt Whitman:

"Well—it's our game; that's the chief fact in connection with it; America's game; it has the snap, go, fling of the American atmosphere; it belongs as much to our institutions, fits into them as significantly as our Constitution's laws; is just as important in the sum total of our historic life."

Ken Burns, whose documentary *Baseball* chronicled the history of the sport, said, "The story of baseball is also the story of race in America, of immigration and assimilation; of the struggle between labor and management, of popular culture and advertising, of myth and the nature of heroes, villains and buffoons; of the role of women and class and wealth in our society."

On a smaller scale, it also is a game treasured for its simplicity and for its tradition. Over the years, baseball

> The fans care most about preserving the integrity of the game.

Opposite:
The game of baseball is considered by many to be a familiar and an integral part of our society and heritage.

has changed less than most games. The rules and equip-ment—even the uniforms—have remained essentially the same. For those who love to read and analyze statistics, it is the perfect game, since it allows for endless comparison of players—even those who performed generations apart.

Professional baseball players are entertainers. They are ordinary human beings who happen to have an extraordi-nary ability in one area. And for that we idolize them, just as we have always idolized athletes. Through television and the newspapers, we know more about athletes than we once did. We know they are not perfect. Still, we love to watch them play. We love to watch them compete.

That much has not changed. As Pulitzer Prize-winning author David Halberstam said, "It is not so much that Joe DiMaggio has gone away, and America is thereby dimin-ished; it is more that in the end he was a great centerfielder and a great hitter, which is at once far more than enough, and yet a great deal less than the myth."

An Obligation to Play?

When the president of the United States stepped forward and expressed an interest in settling the baseball strike, some people applauded; others were appalled. George Will, a syndicated columnist who is also a big baseball fan, wrote, "In a free society government should not, even if it could, save private parties from the consequences of their mismanagement of their institutions, unless their institu-tions are crucial to the social order, which major league baseball is not."

In other words, baseball is just a game. Or is it? When the president chastised the owners and players for acting like spoiled children, and then recommended that Con-gress get involved in their dispute, he was thinking of baseball as a billion-dollar business affecting millions of people. He also was speaking as a fan of the game. There is no question that the American people can live

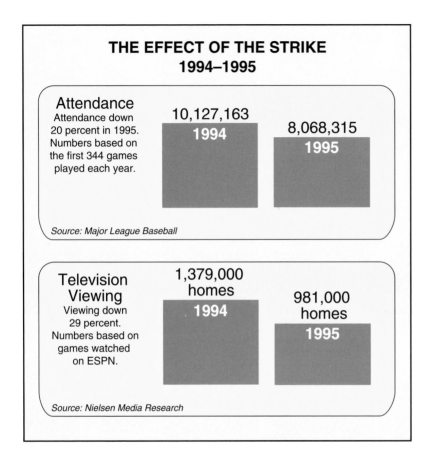

THE EFFECT OF THE STRIKE
1994–1995

Attendance
Attendance down
20 percent in 1995.
Numbers based on
the first 344 games
played each year.

10,127,163
1994

8,068,315
1995

Source: Major League Baseball

Television Viewing
Viewing down
29 percent.
Numbers based on
games watched
on ESPN.

1,379,000 homes
1994

981,000 homes
1995

Source: Nielsen Media Research

without baseball—that much was demonstrated during the strike of 1994. After a while, even the most diehard fans began to fill their time with other activities. Life went on.

But there is no denying that baseball is an important part of American culture, and that its absence was deeply felt. Sadly, though, as the strike dragged on, it appeared to many observers that the fans cared more about the integrity of the game than the owners and players did. Representatives for both sides said they wanted a settlement, but their actions indicated they wanted much more: They wanted complete victory, even if it meant the loss of another season.

Unfortunately, while the owners and players may have had a moral and ethical obligation to set aside their many differences and return to the baseball diamond, they had no legal obligation. So, even as resentment from the public mounted, the strike continued. At stake was not merely the financial security of the owners and players, but the faith and loyalty of the game's fans.

Hope for the Future

One of the strangest things about the strike was the manner in which the league went about its business: While players and owners alternately insulted each other and refused to talk, the league went through with its plans for further expansion. In early March 1995, the Tampa Bay Devil Rays and Arizona Diamond Backs were introduced as the newest franchises in baseball; both will begin play in 1998. Furthermore, teams continued to trade players and sign free agents.

Clearly then, despite the animosity between the two sides, there was evidence that baseball was not dead. At the very least, the people within the game expected to be back on the field sometime in the not-too-distant future.

But that was only part of the equation. What baseball lacked in 1994 and early 1995, was a strong commissioner—someone with the authority to step in and force both owners and players to bargain in good faith. Any lasting peace is virtually impossible without a full-time commissioner whose first concern is for the game of baseball and its fans.

Baseball and labor experts alike also agreed that the game needed a new long-term collective bargaining agreement that would be fair—or equally unfair—to both sides. The idea of victory was ridiculous. A compromise was greatly needed. In that way, the threat of a strike would not hang over the game every few years, as it has for nearly three decades.

On March 26, 1995, the National Labor Relations Board voted to seek an injunction (a court order requiring

Presidential Involvement

When the United States entered World War II in December 1941 after the bombing of Pearl Harbor, there was some question about whether the league should suspend play indefinitely. A number of players had either enlisted or been drafted, and the country as a whole had turned its full attention and energy to the war effort. Among baseball insiders, there was concern that by playing during such a serious time, the league would be showing a lack of respect for American soldiers.

Commissioner Kenesaw Mountain Landis wrote to President Franklin D. Roosevelt, asking his advice. "Baseball is about to adopt schedules, sign players, make vast commitments, go to training camps," he wrote. "What do you want us to do? If you believe we ought to close down for the duration of the war, we are ready to do so immediately. If you feel we ought to continue, we would be delighted to do so. We await your order."

After consulting with his secretary, a baseball fan, Roosevelt wrote a reply to the commissioner:

"I honestly feel that it would be best for the country to keep baseball going. There will be fewer people unemployed and everybody will work longer hours and harder than ever before. And that means that they ought to have a chance for recreation and for taking their minds off their work even more than before."

Roosevelt noted that players of active military age should offer their services to their country. The games, however, should continue. Baseball, he said, was "a recreational asset to at least 20 million people—and that in my judgment is thoroughly worthwhile."

Roughly 340 major leaguers entered the armed services, along with 3,000 minor league players. Only a few big leaguers saw combat duty—most played baseball for the army or navy to raise money and to provide entertainment for the troops.

Back home, teams scrambled to fill their rosters with older players, and the games went on as scheduled.

or forbidding some act) to force owners to restore the terms of baseball's former economic system, including free-agent bidding, salary arbitration, and anti-collusion (a secret agreement for a deceitful purpose) rules. If the injunction was granted, the players indicated they would end the strike immediately and return to the field. The owners, at first, said they would probably appeal to a higher court and threatened to lock the players out if the injunction was granted.

The next day, the two sides went back to the negotiating table. Management made another proposal, this time offering, among other things, to keep the current system of salary arbitration and free agency, or to eliminate arbitration and lower the threshold for unrestricted free agency from six years to four. This sounded good to the players; however, the two sides remained far apart on other issues, including the rate at which a team's payroll and revenue would be taxed.

Just two days later, on March 29, four days before opening day, members of the Major League Players Association voted to end the strike if an injunction was granted. Negotiations continued with a renewed sense of urgency. For the first time in months, it seemed, there was progress. There was hope.

On March 31, U.S. District Judge Sonia Sotomayor ruled in favor of the players and issued an injunction against the owners. Judge Sotomayor ordered management to restore free agent bidding, salary arbitration, and the anti-collusion provisions of the expired collective bargaining agreement.

As far as the players were concerned, the strike ended at that moment. They had promised to return to work if an injunction was granted, and that was what they intended to do. It was not quite that simple, though. There was still the possibility that the owners would lock the players out while the two sides negotiated a new collective bargaining agreement. Opening Day was only two days away, and the prospect of replacement baseball still hung in the air.

On April 2, however, the owners got together for a meeting in New York and agreed to accept the players' offer. Replacement players were sent home, and Bud Selig announced that an abbreviated spring training would begin in a few days. A 144-game season (18 games fewer than usual) would begin on April 26. "It feels good to talk about the season starting, talking about baseball," Selig said. "This is not anything I want to go through again."

But the battle was not yet over. The strike lasted 234 days and cost the baseball industry an estimate $900 million. And, in the end, there was no resolution. The players and owners merely agreed to put their differences aside for a few months and play one more season under the old rules; they still had not established a new collective bargaining agreement. To many observers, this only meant that another work stoppage was quite likely in the near future.

Even though the strike was settled, there was still no guarantee that fans would rush back to the ballparks—although in the past, they always had. The anger had always gone away, and the fans had been willing to forgive and forget. They had bought tickets, programs, and hot

On April 26, 1995, the Colorado Rockies held opening day ceremonies at their home field in Denver. Due to the strike, professional teams would play fewer games during the season.

Baseball Outside America

Baseball is known as America's Pastime, but it is equally popular in other countries. In Cuba and the Dominican Republic, for example, baseball players are national heroes. Much as they do in the United States, children there begin playing at a young age, dreaming of the day when they can take their place in the big leagues.

Perhaps no culture, though, embraces baseball with greater passion than the Japanese. The sport was introduced to Japan in the 1850s; the first professional league was formed in 1935. Japanese baseball has become wildly popular, and the quality of play has improved dramatically. It is not unusual for American baseball stars, particularly those approaching the end of their careers, to seek employment in one of the two Japanese professional leagues: the Central and the Pacific. American players have the skills necessary to compete in Japan; however, they sometimes find it difficult to adjust to a radically different way of life.

As one American player once said about baseball in Japan, "Sure they play with a bat and a ball and with the same rules, but believe me, baseball over there is a whole 'nuther game."

Pride, discipline, and respect are paramount in Japanese baseball. The public outbursts and displays of emotion so common in American sports are frowned upon. Batters, in fact, are expected to bow to umpires. Teams routinely practice for several hours in the afternoon before playing a game at night. In Japanese baseball, tie games are permitted, even encouraged, because a tie prevents either team from experiencing the disgrace of losing.

Ballplayers in Japan stress, above all else, a concept known as *wa*, which means team unity. In contrast, Americans pride themselves on their fierce individualism. In Japan, however, the word for individualism *kojinshugi*, is considered offensive. The most beloved and respected Japanese players are those who are humble and obedient, who understand that it is the manager who knows what is best. Not surprisingly, labor problems are extremely rare in Japanese baseball. A players' union was formed in 1985, but union leader Kiyoshi Nakahata made a point of saying, "We'd never act like the U.S. major leaguers. A strike would be going too far."

Opposite:
Twelve-year-old Tommy VanWolfe holds up a sign expressing some fans' opinion during a game in April 1995. Other fans, however, are finding it difficult to forgive the players for their long absence.

dogs, and they had sat in the stands and applauded and cheered for their heroes.

This dispute was different, though. Never before had a strike lasted so long; never before had a strike wiped out the World Series; never before had the public expressed such anger and outrage. A sign that had been held up at Yankee Stadium just before the strike began in August seemed to echo the feelings of millions of fans:

"The game is perfect. It's the people who screw it up."

Nearly eight months later, the fans still sounded bitter.

"I don't care if I never see another game," said seventy-six-year-old Aldo Giancoli of Philadelphia. "When I heard the strike was over, my response was, 'So what?' I've been

a lifelong baseball fan, and my feeling for the game now is nothing."

If there was cause for optimism, it could be found in the words of the players and coaches, who seemed, finally, to realize what they were in danger of losing.

"The game has taken a beating the past eight months," said Paul O'Neill of the New York Yankees. "We have to take a reality check and realize how lucky we are to be playing."

Chronology

1869 Cincinnati Red Stockings field the first professional baseball team.

1870 National Association of Professional Base Ball Players is formed.

1876 Formation of the eight-team National League of Professional Base Ball Clubs.

1883 "Reserves clauses" become part of all professional contracts.

1889 Owners impose salary limit of $2,500. Angry players respond by breaking off and forming the Players League.

1912 First strike in baseball history. Only time replacement players were ever used. Detroit Tigers used eight replacements and lost to Philadelphia Athletics, 24–2.

1919 Black Sox Scandal. Players on Chicago White Sox team "fixed" the World Series.

1920 Rube Foster launches the Negro National League.

1927 Babe Ruth hits sixty home runs in a single season.

1943 Phillip Wrigley, ruler of the gum empire, launches the All-American Girls Professional Baseball League.

1972 Players strike for thirteen days over the issue of salary arbitration.

1975 Reserve clause dies when an arbitration panel declares pitchers Andy Messersmith and Dave McNally to be free agents.

1981 Players strike for fifty days over the issue of free-agent compensation.

1989 Baseball owners are found guilty of collusion after boycotting 1985–1986 free-agent market.

1992 Commissioner Fay Vincent is forced to resign by team owners.

August 12, 1994 Players go on strike.

September 14, 1994 Acting commissioner Bud Selig announces the cancellation of the World Series.

December 27, 1994 MLBPA submits to the National Labor Relations Board a set of unfair labor practices charges against the owners.

February 14, 1995 Senators Orrin Hatch and Daniel Patrick Moynihan introduce a bill in Congress that would repeal baseball's exemption from antitrust laws.

February 16, 1995	Spring training begins—with replacement players.
March 26, 1995	National Labor Relations Board votes to seek injunction that would restore the terms of baseball's expired collective bargaining agreement.
March 29, 1995	MLBPA members vote to end the strike if an injunction is granted.
March 31, 1995	The strike ends when U.S. District Judge Sonia Sotomayor rules in favor of the players and issues an injunction against the owners ordering them to restore free-agent bidding, salary arbitration, and anti-collusion rules.
April 2, 1995	The owners accept the players' offer to return to work. Replacement players are sent home. Plans for an abbreviated 144-game season are announced.
April 25, 1995	First game of the 1995 professional baseball season.
April 26, 1995	Opening day of the 1995 season for all other teams.

For Further Reading

Adler, David A. *Jackie Robinson: He Was the First.* New York: Holiday House, 1989.

Berke, Art. *Babe Ruth.* New York: Franklin Watts, 1988.

Brashler, William. *The Story of Negro League Baseball.* New York: Ticknor & Fields, 1994.

Greenberg, Keith. *Nolan Ryan.* Vero Beach, FL: Rourke Publications, Inc., 1993.

Helmer, Diana Star. *Belles of the Ballpark.* Brookfield, CT: The Millbrook Press, 1993.

Ritter, Lawrence S. *The Story of Baseball.* New York: William Morrow and Co., 1990.

Index

Adams, Daniel Lucius, 16
African Americans. *See* Blacks.
All-American Girls Professional Baseball League, 25
American Negro League (ANL), 23
Anderson, Sparky, 44, 45
Angelos, Peter, 42–43
Antitrust exemption, 36
Arbitration, salary, 39, 53

Bagwell, Jeff, 6, 8
Belle, Albert, 8
Blacks
   color barrier and, 22, 24
   Negro leagues and, 23
Black Sox Scandal, 18
Bonds, Barry, 8
Bonilla, Bobby, 30
Boston Red Sox, 13
Brotherhood of Professional Base Ball Players, 28–29
Burns, Ken, 49

Cartwright, Alexander, 16
Chicago White Sox, 18
Cicotte, Eddie, 18
Cincinnati Red Stockings, 14, 15, 17, 19, 30
Clinton, Bill, 39, 41, 42
Cobb, Ty, 43, 45
Collective bargaining agreement, 9–10, 31
Commissioner's office, 40
Congress, 36, 50–51
Cricket, 15
Cuba, 56

Darling, Ron, 5

Detroit Tigers, 43–45
Divito, David, 37
Dominican Republic, 56
Doubleday, Abner, 15

Eastern Colored League (ECL), 23

Federal League, 36
Fehr, Donald, 11, 40
Flood, Curt, 31–32
Free agency, 9–10, 27–28, 31–33, 35, 53–54

Gandil, Chick, 18
Gaston, Cito, 42
Gehrig, Lou, 21
Giancoli, Aldo, 56, 58
Graham, Robert, 36
Griffey, Ken, Jr., 5, 6, 7, 8
Gwynn, Tony, 8

Halberstam, David, 50
Hatch, Orrin, 36
Hirtensteiner, Rick, 43
Holmes, Oliver Wendell, Jr., 36
Hornsby, Rogers, 21
Hunter, Jim "Catfish," 33

Jackson, Joe, 18
Japan, 56

Kelly, Mike "King," 29
Kojinshugi, 56
Kuhn, Bowie, 31, 34–35

Landis, Kenesaw Mountain, 18, 40, 53

Maddux, Greg, 9
McNally, Dave, 33
Messersmith, Andy, 33
Miller, Marvin, 31, 32–33
Minor league baseball, 46
Monash, Adam, 13
Moynihan, Daniel Patrick, 36

National Basketball Association (NBA), 6, 10
National Football League (NFL), 6, 10, 47
National Labor Relations Board, 39, 52–53
National League of Professional Base Ball Clubs, 28, 29–30
Negro American League (NAL), 23
Negro leagues, 23
Negro National League (NNL), 23
New York Knickerbocker Base Ball Club, 15–17
New York Yankees, 9, 19, 21

O'Neill, Paul, 58

Paige, Leroy Satchel, 23
Pelegrino, Bob, 13
Players League, The, 29–30
Presidential involvement, 39, 41, 42, 50, 53

Reich, Robert, 41
Replacement baseball, 41–47
Reserve clause, 28, 31, 33
Revenue sharing, 9, 10–11
Revolving, 27

Rickey, Branch, 22
Ripken, Cal, Jr., 8–9
Robinson, Jackie, 22, 24
Rogers, Kenny, 9
Rokos, George, 13
Roosevelt, Franklin D., 53
Rose, Pete, 34
Rounders, 15
Ruth, George Herman
    "Babe," 19–21, 30

Salaries, increase in, 28, 30
Salary arbitration, 39, 53
Salary cap, 9–10, 29, 39

Selig, Bud, 12, 13, 40
Sullivan, Joseph, 18

Television revenues
    increase in, 11
    revenue sharing and, 11
Thomas, Frank, 6, 8
Town ball, 15

Ueberroth, Peter, 40
Usery, W.J., 38, 39, 41, 43

VanWolfe, Tommy, 56, 57

Vendors, 13
Vincent, Fay, 40

Wa, 56
Ward, John Montgomery,
    26, 27, 28
Whitman, Walt, 49
Will, George, 50
Williams, Claude "Lefty," 18
Women, baseball league for, 25
Wright, George, 30
Wright, Harry, 17, 19
Wrigley, Phillip, 25

Acknowledgments and photo credits

Cover: ©Steve Ross/Leo de Wys, Inc.; p. 4: ©Frank White/Liaison International; p. 7: ©Sam Jones/Gamma Liaison; pp. 8, 12, 24, 32, 37, 43, 55, 57: ©AP/Wide World Photos; p. 13: ©S. Silverman/ Gamma Liaison; pp. 14, 16–17, 18, 20, 21, 23, 25, 26, 32, 34, 44: National Baseball Library & Archive, Cooperstown, NY; p. 31: Bettmann Archive; pp. 36, 40: ©Terry Ashe/Gamma Liaison; p. 38: Cynthia Johnson/Gamma Liaison; p. 42: ©Dirck Halstead/Gamma Liaison; pp. 46, 48: ©Bruce Glassman/Blackbirch Press, Inc.

Charts and graphs by Blackbirch Graphics, Inc.